DROUGHT RESISTANT STRAIN

Drought Resistant Strain

Mather Schneider

INTERIOR NOISE PRESS
Austin, TX

DROUGHT RESISTANT STRAIN
Copyright © 2010 by Mather Schneider

All rights reserved. Printed in the United States of America. No part of this book may be used or reproduced in any manner whatsoever without written permission except in the case of brief quotations embodied in critical articles and reviews.

For order information and current mailing address please visit
www.interiornoisepress.com

Interior Noise Press
P.O. Box 17084
Austin, TX 78760

Cover Art by Mather Schneider

Library of Congress Control Number: 2009942358

ISBN 978-0-9816606-1-5

First Edition

for Ara

Contents

ME AND JOSIE GO TO THE ZOO	13
HOUSE ACROSS THE ALLEY	14
CROOKED	15
LAZY SUNDAY AFTERNOON	16
108 DEGREE RUSH HOUR	17
ATTITUDE	18
THE WISDOM OF WHISPERIN' RON	19
JULIE AT THE BASHFUL BANDIT	20
THE BARRIER	21
THE BEETLE WALKS IN CIRCLES	22
OLD TIMERS	23
WATCHING A SNAKE EAT A BIRD	24
YOU CAN'T GET AWAY FROM NATURE	25
LONG PERIOD EVENT	26
HEADLOCKS	27
CURVES CABARET	28
THE NATURE OF THE OOZING MATERIAL	29
THESE SPLAYED NERVES	30
MONDAY	31
AFTER CROSSING THE BORDER AT NOGALES	32
WITHDRAWAL	33
THE PROBLEM WITH COMMUNES	34
THE CLOCK HAND MOVES	35
THE CARPENTER	36
SHIM	37
WHERE NOTHING GREW EXCEPT LEGENDS	38
OUR TIN ROOF	39

WE ARE	40
THE BUTTERFLY EFFECT	41
LA LLORONA	42
THE TRAVELING SHOW	43
NAP NIGHTMARE	44
THE FENCE	45
OLD GENE	46
A LONG WAY FROM BLUEBERRY HILL	47
WHEN IT COMES TO HOOKERS	48
MY HAT IS STARTING TO STINK	49
OUR LAST SUNSET	50
THE SELF MEDICATER	51
A SERIOUS PIECE	52
VASELINA AND COMPANY	53
REMINDER	54
CAT'S CLAW	55
LESSON	56
BONITA FAMILIA	57
WASH	58
THAT AWKWARD AGE	59
DWAYNE	60
IMBECILES IN THE TORRENT	61
NAKED PREGNANT EVIL CLOWN FACE	62
HOT IRON	64
SHARON	65
TUCSON MONSOON	66
EARLY/LATE	67
I STICK TO THE DAY	68
BETWEEN US AND IT	69

THE RUG	70
AFTER VISITING JOSIE'S FAMILY IN MEXICO	71
AT THE PARK	72
THE LAST WILL AND TESTICLE	73
THREE WEEKS I'LL NEVER GET BACK	75
BILL COLLECTOR	76
THE BELL	77
THE JAGS	78
ON THE OTHER SIDE OF THE MOUNTAIN	79
WE'VE ALWAYS BEEN A FAMILY DOLLAR FAMILY	80
SAM	81
FRAGILE	82
THE BUFFET TAVERN, TUCSON, ARIZONA	83
TRASH	84
THE COPPERHEAD AND THE BLUE FLOWER	85
BAD SUMMER	86
HALF DRUNK IN THE AFTERNOON	87
I WISH I HAD SOME ROPE	88
COUNTY	89
BOO	90
NEW YEAR'S EVE	91
THINGS CAN BE BEAUTIFUL EVEN WHEN THEY'RE NOT	92
WE HAVE SEEN IT FOR SO LONG	94
GERTRUDE THE GOOD	95
LA DUEÑA	96
4 AMERICAN MEN SIT AT THE CAMPGROUND PICNIC TABLE DRINKING BEER	97
BULIMIA	98
THIS GIRL	99
HOT AIR BALLOON RIDE	100

BATH DAY	101
SPRING IS IN THE AIR	102
THE STRAYS	103
DEEDER OF THE DAMNED	104
IT SEEMS IMPOSSIBLE	105
ON THE CORNER OF MAPLE AND EUCLID	106
ONCE YOU'VE PAID	107
JAMIE	108
OUTHOUSE	109
THE MINUTES TIGHT WITH REPENTANCE	110
TONYA WEISS	111
MY LAST LUCKY PENNIES	112
SHOOTING THE CHICKENS	113
DRIVING HOME FROM MY MOM'S FUNERAL	114
AN ANGEL IN AN ANKLE BRACELET	115
GONE	116
THANKSGIVING 2002	118
THAT SWEET PLACE	119
FAMILY TREE	120
SCUBA DIVING IN LA PAZ	121
THE YEAR OF THE MOREL	123
TEN YEARS AWAY	124

There is a crack in everything God has made.

Ralph Waldo Emerson

ME AND JOSIE GO TO THE ZOO

I can't speak Spanish
and she can't speak English
so me and Josie go to the zoo.
It's easy not to talk
while watching the rhinos,
their heads like prehistoric toolboxes
and bodies like boulders
carved with petroglyphs,
or the bears,
half insane with sitting there
like patched toys
never to smile,
or the giant cats pacing
so pissed,
so pissed.
The lemurs have more words in common
than we do
as we stroll the path
between the man made worlds
with every rough patch glued together
with kisses.
This is the magic:
that we can't see it coming.
All evolution and all time
have prepared for this moment,
have prepared for us
to be here now
like this,
just as it has prepared for the peregrine
to escape his rope
and attack a child,
and for the trainer to stand
with mouth agape,
and for the monkeys to scream
and beat their cages.

HOUSE ACROSS THE ALLEY

It hurts to begin with
and then hurts more to
have no word for it.

Squash-yellow curtains
curl in the windowpanes
that cry when they're broken.

In the asylum of the garden
an old woman mumbles
to her blooming candelilla

and a dog materializes
at the chain-link, but don't
trust his smile.

CROOKED

I'd just moved in to Two Palms Court
and I parked my car kind of crooked
outside my apartment.
I was drinking coffee and looking out the window
when the old neighbor lady came sneaking over
and began examining my car.
I went outside as she was about to
open the car door.
"Can I help you?" I said.
"Oh," she said, "well I saw this car here, and,
I mean I noticed it parked
here, this way, like this,
and I just wondered why
anyone would park this way,
I mean, you know, when there's all this
space?"
"I don't know," I said,
"I'm new here."
"I just couldn't," she said,
"figure it out."
"Maybe you should stop trying to," I said.
She backed away
and retreated to her slit blinds.
Later I learned
this old lady's daughter
owns the whole apartment building.
In fact she owns half of Tucson, it seems,
and she still lets her mother sleep
in a slum.

LAZY SUNDAY AFTERNOON

Baseball game's on
and it's another hot one out
there.

Arizona summer days
nosebleed winds
purple dust
pollution
pollen in the allergen air

make for quite a
sunset.

Earlier
a girl stopped by
just to
have sex.

She wasn't wearing
underwear
was slightly
drunk
and afterwards
she just got up
and left.

Nothing like the sound
of a baseball
game
after a day like
that.

My team's
losing
and I don't
care.

108 DEGREE RUSH HOUR

On the radio talkshow the topic is cloned young.
A traffic helicopter flups
over the choked blacktop

and dogs loll from stuck trucks
like gargoyles slobbering
onto the broiled road.

There is death in our getaway,
in the blood-red arrow,
in the merge

like a leap of faith,
in the freeway ramp spiraling like DNA.
We can only hope to move

a little at a time,
and to spot the cop
before the prick in the Jag.

Dumbfounding the infinite variety
of the middle finger.
Above the surface streets

the wires sag
like tired musical bars
whose notes fold their wings in the smog.

ATTITUDE

2 young thugs moved into
apartment #41
in the middle of the night.
All they ever did
was sit by their window
and carve things into their arms
with hunting knives.
Then last week
one of them asked Ken,
who lives in #37,
if they could borrow his car
to take their mother
to the hospital.
Ken had just watched
a *Power of Positive Thinking* video,
and so he said yes.
After a day and a half he
knew he'd never see them or
the car again.
But he wasn't going
to let life get him down.
He remembered the video.
He broke into their apartment.
It smelled like rotten food
and there were sunflower seeds
all over the floor.
There was nothing of value
except a pair of roller blades
in the closet.
They were 3 sizes too big
but Ken put them on
anyway, tied them as tight
as he could,
and skated back and forth
on the sidewalk
all day.

THE WISDOM OF WHISPERIN' RON

Little Peggy, the bartender, is eighty years old,
but the Bashful Bandit is slow
at six-thirty a.m.
She waddles out of the back room
and sets down a big bowl of grapes on the bar
in front of Whisperin' Ron
like a still life in the half light.
Whisperin' Ron had a cancer operation on his throat
ten years ago when he
turned fifty,
and now he talks in a hoarse loud whisper.
He puts his cigarette and beer down
and carefully picks out a grape.
"Freshly washed and chilled," Peggy says.
Whisperin' Ron puts the grape
into his mouth and chews thoughtfully
with obvious pleasure
for a long time.
"Mmmmmm, mmmmm, mmmmmmmm..."
Then he swallows like a pelican.
"You know what, Peggy?" he whispers.
"What, dear?" Peggy says,
leaning her ear toward him.
"Grapes make great wine," he says.
He smiles very big and sits back.
"Yes they do, dear," Peggy says,
"Yes they certainly do."

JULIE AT THE BASHFUL BANDIT

Your cigarette smoke curls up
like a telephone cord
to the hereafter.

Over the oval maw of a highball
a wan smile rims
a red straw.

Your hands
are like crazy
white spiders

and your drinks
are a long line of buckets
leading to a fire.

THE BARRIER

I am a lost idiot
running around naked
with sticky fingers, nearly mute,
an infant using sign.
I want to kiss now

and chat later,
I want to use my tongue
to do and undo everything
like a hair wagging the tail
or a letter jumping back

onto a typewriter ribbon.
Everything is backwards, señorita,
or I wish it were. I'm too old
to feel like such a child
standing next to you.

You smile at my dumb sounds,
my jerkiness, the smallest
of all small talk. I try
to make my eyes clever
but you see right through me

to the truth of a shy boy.
Your voice is a song
I don't know the words to,
but you are afraid to say my name,
and I am afraid to say yours.

THE BEETLE WALKS IN CIRCLES

You comply and comply
as if there is no alternative
only the variable sameness
and voices from the rooms of souls
lilt like elevator music
as the beetle walks in circles on a
summer night
around the arrogance of the thinker
who can't outwit death
who understands nothing but self importance
as the proud conqueror
crushes his boot into an anthill
lacquered monsters crawl
the hirsute epoch
ozone musk means nothing
to philosophy
the pheromones of hells and hatreds
await new meaning
love is coming
but does not look like you
have pictured in your
mind.

OLD TIMERS

My grandparents
are getting old.
They stopped sleeping
in the same bed
a long time ago.
Now they don't even sleep
in the same room.
I don't know
if they are still in love
or if they
ever were.
You get the feeling they're
beyond all that.
Each morning
whoever wakes up first
gets out of bed
and shuffles across the house
to see if the other
is still alive
before starting the
coffee.

WATCHING A SNAKE EAT A BIRD

The neck flexes and
inches forward
like rubber pantyhose over
the pretty head.
As it expands the scales
separate on the mouth
and the tiny red cracks
of the veins
leap as the skin
is pulled like a tide
smothering rib
by rib
toward the feet kicking
like a drowning man trying to get
out of a straight jacket:
feathers lathered with saliva,
underwater screams,
each instant dovetailing
into the void
like the empty space you left
last spring.
When it's over there are only two
yellow eyes
split by black lightning
and a lump
in the gut
that still kicks
sometimes.

YOU CAN'T GET AWAY FROM NATURE

She used to categorize her orgasms
as flowers:
a rose was the very best,
then lilac, daffodil, daisy...
This sounds dandy
except mine was not the little joy
of a hummingbird
poking his beak into a larkspur,
no, I worked
for those orgasms:
I had to start from scratch,
undoing her botany
and everything else she'd been taught,
easing it up
through the hardpan,
hauling the water,
performing feats of endurance
with tongue or hand.
I've sweated less working peat into the ground
with a shovel.
One hot day I explained to her
the type of flower she had
was due to the length of my
servitude down there,
and I'd rather settle
for a dandelion
than dislocate an elbow.
We split up after that.
I don't know what kind of farmer
she finally landed.
You can't get away from nature.
Two months later
I met a biker chick
who grew her own weed.

LONG PERIOD EVENT

I sat on the kitchen floor while the water
glass scooted toward the edge
of the counter as if on the shoulders
of ants.
A minor earthquake,
nothing like what happened years before
inside my father's skull.
If that same tremor had come through
when I was eight
in the hospital with my mother,
while my father lay unconscious,
I would not have noticed.
I already staggered with each step and
the walls already flowed like lava.
My father never woke up and there
wasn't any brand new world
fresh and steaming from the smelter of dawn
and I didn't understand
that we are all imperfect,
but that nothing is wrong with us.
And then one day I was an old man
and the world shivered
and I fell on the kitchen floor
like a rag doll.
When everything was still again
I stayed there
thinking of him
and of other things,
looking at that water glass stopped
on the precipice.

HEADLOCKS

I met the Masked Marvel the other day.
He was drinking whiskey at three in the afternoon
at the Golden Nugget. He was seventy-four years old,
everyone called him Doc.

Years ago he was a traveling professional wrestler
moving from town to town, grappling with The Predator
and Chainsaw Charlie.
It was quite a life drinking
from ship-sized barrels of rum,
a new bone or joint cracked and twisted each day.
He told me he still had his leather mask
and shoulder pads.

Life was real back then, he said,
mapping out his countless scars.
He had been beaten and come back for more, somehow
enjoying it, the animal victories
of rubbing men's faces into the mat, the blood-thirst
of the crowd. He thought it a lucky game
and he fancied himself a winner, even as he downed
shot after shot.
When he stood to go to the bathroom the bartender
told me Doc was a vet, a few rounds
short of a clip, usually harmless, but if he tried to demonstrate
any of his old moves on me it
was suggested that I leave.

I thought about the other man, the unlucky one
who holds everything in his whole life
until he snaps, unleashing bullets into the ring
of the Circle K. I pictured him forever pinned
against the ropes of madness,
whispering pleads to cauliflower-eared walls
costumed in a straight jacket.

When he returned from the bathroom
I turned and looked at the Masked Marvel, old Doc
and raised my glass to the pain.

CURVES CABARET

Pat down blues

lunch hour chow buffet

the bartender in her panties

pink and yellow matches
in a bucket on the bar
like sulphur candies in the blacklight

everything glowing like our blue smiling teeth

the waitresses holding their round trays
above their heads like halos

dancers Amber Alexis Summer Twilight Larissa
knowing nothing can touch them here

the white shirts of the bouncers
fluttering like moth-angels

a DJ called BB
spinning beat with no soul
from some gothic ceiling-world
of threesomes and suicide

lapdancers reconnoitering the room
with eyes you turn away from
like beggars on the street

the cold geometry of the stage

the will of the fireman's pole.

THE NATURE OF THE OOZING MATERIAL

Ray has a weeping hole in the back of his head.
He thinks a spider bit him.
The hole is about the size of a penny
and his hair is matted up around it.
Ray is thirty-eight years old,
about five feet tall with his cowboy boots on
and maybe a hundred pounds
with his knife on his belt.
Ray takes pills to sleep
and pills to wake up,
he takes pills before he eats
and pills after,
he takes pills for depression and anxiety
and ADHD.
His stomach, pancreas and bowels
are shot,
he has Crohn's Disease,
chronic asthma and allergies,
he messes his pants sometimes
and drinks 12 cans of soda a day.
And now he's got this
hole in the back of his head.
He sticks his finger in it and tries to understand
the nature of the oozing material
that stains his pillow in the night.
He doesn't know what's
happened to him.
He drives a cab and stays
with his ma.

THESE SPLAYED NERVES

are like rat nails
running across your face in the night,
like scared beetles scratching
the drums of your gut-ears,
like the split red tongues of an acre of snakes
rising straight up
to look you in the eye.
These splayed nerves are like the bloodshot veins
of leaves shaking and halfway eaten
by a worm
that will never be a butterfly.
These splayed nerves take everything
in its time,
all this life and half life,
all this anxiety like wet silk
burning in the colon.
The teachers try to calm,
they teach people not to think too much
or to worry
but if the teachers don't have splayed nerves
that jump like grubby corn
under the skin of their soul,
then the teachers don't know.
These splayed nerves don't want
to heal themselves
or to agree
on what has been agreed upon,
what can't be understood,
they want to fly apart
each in a new direction.
They want to love up to the moment
of the fracturing,
but no further.

MONDAY

I walked to work this morning
in the 5 a.m. dark.

Outside the locked liquor store
at Glenn and First
a young guy in dirty clothes
jumped out of the dumpster
like a Jack-in-the-box.

He stood there looking at me.
He brought his hands to his head
and pulled his hair.
His movements were exaggerated
and his legs were
juiced rubber.

His face was like a tree knot
and he started screaming:
"Dead body! Dead body!
There's a dead body in there!"

He walked in fast circles
staring at the dark green
city dumpster.

He slapped his hands against
his thighs and stomach.
He grunted and howled and moaned.

As I walked over to the dumpster
and looked in
the guy screamed and ran
away into the darkness.

The dumpster was empty:
no dead body.

I was almost
disappointed.

AFTER CROSSING THE BORDER AT NOGALES

we can breathe again.

Driving home through Arizona
her Mexican divorce papers in the glove
she holds tight to me and to the promise
of making money
like two porpoise-dreams pulling her
through a river of uselessness.

She's small and dark and lovely
and kind, and we can hardly speak to each other
but it doesn't matter.

So what if love
is a lie
where we agree to meet?

She feeds me pieces of banana with her little
terra cotta fingers
and laces the air with a silver-toothed smile
and tosses the greasy yellow peel
onto the shoulder of the highway
while I drive under the raw Sonoran sun
and butcher my Spanish to tell her
what I think is important in life,
which doesn't take long:
letting go of shame.
We have agreed, we have
decided, we have been swept away
while letting ourselves,
and we have, somehow, slipped
through.

WITHDRAWAL

I walk the 3 miles to the university
and slide my sackful of overdue books
down the chute.

Their books are too thick
their books are
too self satisfied
their books are too
tired.

What a strange game of
more and more and more we
play.

Kids play frisbee on the bottled grass
and professors quick-walk
across brick commons dusted red
like old gray birds
that can't fly.

This is a horrible place:
they want to train me
to be like them.

I feel too much
this sandpaper sameness
and maybe I am insane but
I have to go:

their books are too heavy and
do not give me
what I need.

THE PROBLEM WITH COMMUNES

My parents found out what was wrong
with the idea of a commune
when they moved to Arkansas
with another family.

We lived out in the woods
four miles from our nearest neighbor
our driveway was a creek bed
and our house was an old
barely renovated barn.

We had a garden
made our own lye soap
bathed in the creek
raised chickens
goats
pigs.

It was nice
for the summer
but it couldn't last.

The problem with communes is
you end up fucking the other
man's wife
or slapping
the other man's child

and it is hard to keep secrets
in a life without walls.

The problem with communes is
the people.

THE CLOCK HAND MOVES

like a lizard stalking
a fly
it will never catch.
Ask the old man
folded over
a cardboard sign
on the final asphalt
island
at Douglas and Valencia,
three lanes of rush
hour madness on either side,
his only shade
the prison bar
cast from the light pole
that moves slowly across
his sopping body.
Or ask the stray cat
at your back door at
4 a.m.
when you're alone
and you can't sleep,
when yesterday is two hundred miles
of bad road behind you
and tomorrow
is a ball of tinfoil
wrapped around a dollar bill and
buried on the moon.
They will both
tell you the same
sad story.

THE CARPENTER

I started an argument with Karen
and kicked a hole in her deck.
We had been dating for two weeks
and that night we had sex
for the first time.
In the morning
she told me not to worry
about the deck
and the next day it was fixed like magic.
It turned out her neighbor
was a carpenter.
She always bragged about him
about how nice he was
and how good he was.
It wasn't until three years later
when we were breaking up
that I found out she'd been sleeping with him
and continued to sleep with him
for a long time after
in exchange for little
chores.
At the end
we ripped each other apart
like a couple of dogs
insulting everything the other
believed in or cared about.
But of all the things we said
what haunts me most
is that carpenter
with no face
and her legs
spread for
him.

SHIM

The spider purrs
and vibrates in the fulcrum
of the teeter-totter
while the moth spasms
in his silk straight jacket.

A few feet away
a young girl pushes her little sister
on the swing.

I remember the first time
I went so high on a swing
the chains buckled. That little

stomach lurching delay.

Between falling
in and out of love
there is a pinnacle,
but remembering itself
can be a kind
of height sickness.

A man is a shim
between two cold fastnesses

and life is an interlude
like a sudden and brief torchlight
before our faces are buried
in the blackness

with its tarantula
fingers.

WHERE NOTHING GREW EXCEPT LEGENDS

Mom tossed an old tomato
out by the edge of the woods
and suddenly there was a giant bush

burning with fruit. We were grateful,
but you can only eat and can
so many tomatoes.

We had enough tomatoes to get rid of
a point-blank skunk spray.
So we waited for that.

Worse than our red stained hands,
the attar of rotting tomatoes
got into our dreams at night.

I had a dream we set fire to it.
The smell was like burning hair
and the sound like the popping of bones.

OUR TIN ROOF

The squirrels ran around up there
like crazy step-brothers scraping their nails
on the inside of an attic door.
Birds straddled the peak,
their delicate steps
an itch you couldn't scratch.
Even snakes got up there—
someone rubbing calloused hands together
far above us.
In autumn leaves fell on our tin roof,
little bat-wing whispers
brushing your skin,
and the acorns were thrown
from the macabre
parade float oaks.
Rain became music
that would drown you,
and snow was like being buried alive:
it piled up and made a sound
like the earth itself moving.
The wind was the worst,
the way it howled and tore
at the ragged tin tongues,
the way it found and infected each
new crack,
the way it taught us
to raise our voices
louder and louder.

WE ARE

a smoldering
of the oldest symbol
and every morning the alarm goes off
and we get up and do it again
and the sad and beaten sit
in church on Sundays
crying like cats at
the doorways of strangers.
Some people live too long
and others die on the cross
and morality is the last hieroglyph
on the last hill.
I want to be aroused
in the hour of no cities,
the placental flame gulping
the dark,
eyes staring into it
like animals
on the precipice of insight,
a strange hot wind
in my face.

THE BUTTERFLY EFFECT

Josie and I hike up to Finger Rock.
At four thousand feet we see a butterfly
yellow and black and big as my hand
coming right at us
like a dive bomber.
Josie shrieks and jumps
behind me
and I jump too and we both
nearly fall off the cliff
down into the tiny river
winding around down there
like a blue nerve through gristle.
The crash and froth of the earth's blood
can be heard over the pound
of our hearts in our ears
and the white-water vein
flows right through the center
of my stomach
where it's so light my arms reach out
like blind wings of gold powder
in the shovel-mirror sun.
I am in love for the first time
since I wrapped myself up
in a cocoon of dry saliva
and hung for ten years high in a tree with
black branches
like the brittle fingers
of men burnt alive.
The butterfly dances with us
for a moment
then gracefully and clumsily
saunters away
out over the side where the mountain
ends
and the air
begins.

LA LLORONA

She walks across a desert on fire
head held high in the flames
like homicidal poppies

advancing over the mesa, over the milkweed
and the cacti boiling sap.
Smoke cancers the sky

like a hell-cloud inhaling: smell
the burning hair of the cholla
and the down of the owl's clover, see that death

is indigenous, feel the heat
of the melting anemone, the snapdragon's hope,
the broomrape's pride and the wind

whipping in the scorpion weed.
The burning desert glazes
the sand to mirror

but she crosses it,
collecting larkspur
and blazing stars.

THE TRAVELING SHOW

Mama Cat brings her three kittens
around in the mornings.
I watch them play in the bushes
for a while.
They attack each other and Mama too.
Mostly Mama just eyes them proudly or
indifferently and
smacks them if they get too rowdy.
I lean down like a falling
statue
and pour milk into the
dirty bowl in the shade.
They bounce up to me like
new tennis balls.
I can touch them sometimes
like this
as they are lapping it up
if I'm careful and
gentle
they are small and soft
like trembling flowers.
When every drop is gobbled up
they tumble away
through the fence
a traveling show
bidding farewell to the local
suckers.

NAP NIGHTMARE

Somebody's television mumbles through the stucco
that separates us
from the animals.
You are led to the middle of the desert
and left there
like a donkey
wearing blinders.
You don't know
that soon you'll wake up
and laugh.
You think you'll die
right there
in the hot dry dirt.
You think the birds
will peck your bones
to shine in the sun
like beacons.

THE FENCE

There's a shake and splinter
of fenceboard
and jowly gums flapping
pink as worm-belly.
A single canine flashes in the sun
and then a forepaw
like a mole's blind head
and then its twin
churning like pistons.
Then the whole head
smiling dog-face obsessed and deranged
with a single idea,
slimy and struggling
to be born.
When he finally squeezes through his mouse hole
he stands up and shakes himself off
and trots around the parking lot
that is the other side of the world.
It's no paradise
only a paved place
of strange smells and hostile sounds
and after an hour fighting
to get here
in five minutes he returns
to the hole and squirms
back to the familiar.
There are several similar
holes in the fence
where history has repeated
and the owner has bellowed and kicked
and nailed wooden crosses
over them.

OLD GENE

Some people don't like to sit next to him
because he drools.
He's 86
and every day at 3:30
the bartender pours
a scotch and water,
sets it on the bar. Soon
the door will open and the sun will stream in
and here will come old Gene
being pushed in his wheelchair
by the lucky regular
(the duty means a free beer).
He will help Gene up, scoot
him in just right, fold up the wheelchair
and put it in the back room.
Then Gene will pick at a napkin
and stare into the bar
until his second drink, at which point
he'll buy a bag of potato chips
and eat them slowly, little bites
out of each chip.

When he's had 4 drinks
someone will get out the chair
and put him into it,
and then open the door
and back him out into the setting sun.
He always smiles and waves as he goes out backwards
like a mechanical parade float.

He lives right across the street
from the bar
and he's got a pretty good thing going
if you don't think about it too much.

A LONG WAY FROM BLUEBERRY HILL

A large truckload of manure
was dumped in our maintenance lot
to use as soil enrichment
and after the truck was gone
all of us grounds workers stood
marveling at it.

The steam and smoke from the heat
rose up like a volcano
on the hot Tucson summer day.
Lenny and Girard got excited
over the fact that if you could harness
the energy from one of these babies
you could blow up the entire city.

Thomas said he could make a bomb out
of crap and a ping pong ball.

Mike told us how
he had seen a pile of straw and manure
get so hot it caught fire
and burned a barn in half
and almost killed his grandpop.

I just stared at it
and rubbed my palms
on my jeans.

It's a sad situation
when the arrival of a 12 foot high
mountain of shit
is the highlight of your day.

WHEN IT COMES TO HOOKERS

there's no such thing
as a baker's dozen.
I got close to a free one
one time.
Dove came over on my birthday
when I turned
thirty-eight.
She was a call girl from the paper
who I'd known before.
When we were through
she got up and I pushed
the money towards her.
"I thought this was a free one
for your birthday," she said.
"I don't remember you
saying anything like that," I said,
withdrawing
the bills slightly.
"I didn't?" she said.
"I thought I did," she said.
"Oh well," she said.
Then she took the bills
put them in her purse
and walked out the door.

MY HAT IS STARTING TO STINK

It's summer and the sweat
flows like clam juice
and I am sick to my stomach
after being cruel.

My lungs sting like hornets
and outside the oven-breath noon
coughs in its flak jacket
as petrified drivers hang

caught like fish fossils.
It is hard to sympathize sometimes
it is easier to let go
to fall from concrete mountain

to concrete sea
the self and all those others swimming
in the banal sand of absurdity
tripping on emotions like shoelaces
lost in the mess
of family
and the myopia of the brain-body.

Fear pulls like gravity in the blackness
with just a spark of time
to see by
each moment bursting like a pomegranate
in a mind-propeller
until the splatter
makes sense
or it doesn't.

OUR LAST SUNSET

We underestimate everything
and have to scramble up a ragged crest to catch it
nesting down over the cliffs
of the thirsty Sonoran,
a million Saguaro cacti in salute
tall and sentinal over the crimson mesa
like an army on Mars,
dancers in a thousand year dance,
changelings writhing slower than starfish
on a beach with no ocean
in a myth with spines you can touch,
torments silhouetted against the torched orb of time
ebbing like an orange,
infinite forms of infinite courage,
birds born and put to rest in the elders' eyes,
ribs expanding like accordions
in the scarlet creeper wind,
long shadows snaking slowly inland
swallowing rocks and irony and red dust smooth and whole
as melancholy water,
like the open mouth of the soul
and its black reflection,
arms digging into the impossible ground of the past
and thrown up into the last pure rose-milk tear
of tomorrow.
We sit on a rock belched from a volcano
a million years ago
and she stretches away from me into the desert
like a lengthening shadow
and says, "There is no logic
in what we're doing."
We sit in silence until my hands
turn cold and white from the moon
and my pockets come alive
with scorpions.

THE SELF MEDICATER

The blue flame of the lighter
sizzles on the tiny slag heap
that was scraped from the stem
and placed in the bowl, wiped there
like a thick black salve.
The smell of fried chicken comes from somewhere
on the fifth of July
in Tucson, Arizona.
Green tea and locusts and one
hundred ten degrees.
Another story on the news about some richie
shot dead in a hotel room.
He waits
like a pitcher plant
with his toxin-filled bathtub,
his nerve-veined leaves, his trembling
roots.
The wind dries their skin
and leaves the selfsame resin,
and yet they claim they don't know
or understand each other,
two who once whispered in the night
and knew each other's bodies
like blind people.
There is nothing else to do but wait
for time to do
its thing.
He closes his eyes
and the blood leaps in
the darkness.

A SERIOUS PIECE

"D'you wanna piece of me?"
she said.

Yes, I want a piece of you.

I want a piece of shoulder
smooth and white as eggnog
a piece of belly
waving like a flag.

I want a piece of jaw
a piece of neck
from way around back
a piece of collarbone
to savor the wingspan of surrender.

I want long hard pieces
of both lips
a piece of rib cage
(remember the feeling
when I slip it out)
a piece of heart
leaping like a marlin.

I want a piece of what is hidden
a piece of wild eyelid
a piece of each knee
round as baseballs in my hands.

I want a piece of your cry.

I want a piece carved out
and left on me
to dry in the window's breeze.

I want the piece
you have saved for me.

VASELINA AND COMPANY

She was 86'd from The Mint
for hawking blow jobs
and now she comes into The Deadwood every day
to trawl our happy hour.
The reason they call her "Vaselina"
is because she has a constant outbreak of open sores
on the skin of her chin
and she keeps it coated with Vaseline,
thick waves of it
like fallen meringue.
Her chin shines and sparkles in the bar lights
as she glances around
trying to look demure
instead of like something revealed
at low tide.
She's about forty and slim
and seems to be educated
and despite the fact that you can see yourself
in the glisten of her chin
I admit I've
thought about it,
just like Fat Paul who
works down at Pep Boys
and Lenny
who's four-foot-eight
and furry as a wolf.

REMINDER

Today there was a letter in my mailbox
with some other guy's name on it
but my address.
I always open such letters
in case there's any cash inside.
There was nothing but a note
from the University of Arizona
reaffirming their intentions
to study his body after death.
They were just writing
to see if there has been any
change in his health.
This isn't a joke.
I looked at the envelope again
and wondered where he had moved to
or if he was still alive.
Then I threw the letter away
along with the Shopper
and the missing kids.

CAT'S CLAW

My dad's got cat's claw
crawling up the wall
of his mind.
These sixty years
like sixty vines
closing in
ripping him apart
with a grip like a centipede
thick as my wrist.
I love him less and more
every day
and fear the same
for myself:
stuck by a million stingers
of regret
and darkness closing in
like black sorrow
filled
with shaved glass.
My dad's got cat's claw
crawling up the wall
of his mind.
He will soon be poked
clean through
and covered
in leaves.

LESSON

It's cold and rainy out there
in the desert
between everything

and everything else,
as I wonder what to do
to feed stomach and soul.

Airplanes buzz overhead like wasps
doing what nature ensures
they can't help doing.

That's not nature's way,
I think. That's man's way.
How can human beings

be separable from nature?
Nature is a hell of a thing:
right and wrong and in between

all move on together.
I asked a Vietnam vet one time
why we keep going to war,

why we can't learn our lesson.
"Simple," he said.
"War is fun."

BONITA FAMILIA

Carmen's husband is an American Mexican
but Carmen is an illegal Mexican
so when they got in a fight
he called the border patrol
and they deported her
leaving their baby with him.

She tried to come back again
paid somebody a grand to smuggle her across the border
but when she got to her meeting place
in Nogales
the police were there waiting for her.

She tried again
with someone else's identification this time
and she made it
and is now back in Tucson.

She and her husband have made up
and everything's bueno.
She called my girlfriend yesterday
to see if she wanted to have lunch
at the mall.

WASH

There are too many fliers
on the laundromat bulletin board:
bike for sale
lost dog named Wendy
inner fortitude yoga class...
I want to take them all down
and start clean.
I used to do my laundry at my girlfriend's
but you know how that goes.
There's the viscera,
swirling,
turtlenecks and underwear
calmly bombarding the glass.
There's my reflection.
At the end it is a whole lot
of nothing. Ho-
hum, we mine
for quarters, we sit, we watch
a square in the floor.
We pretend
to read.
We wait.

THAT AWKWARD AGE

I like to be outside on a summer night
when my parents are talking

on the picnic table below
the lightning-scarred pine tree, with work

set aside, in the crease
between roars of disappointment

and snoring in a narrow bed,
in that sluiced-heart margin

of cricketsong air,
drinking beer or wine,

their cigarette cherries
dancing with the fireflies

and me out in the woods
alone at that point

where I can hear their voices
but one step farther

and I cannot, walking
that tight rope.

DWAYNE

Dwayne invents a perpetual motion machine
while servicing the physics room.
He's a janitor at the college.
He studies the numbers abandoned
on the blackboard
before erasing them
like a human windshield wiper.
His idea: an immortal generator
with unlimited,
unpolluting energy.
No more killing each other,
no more working two jobs,
no more worrying all the time...
It's simple, all he needs is an ocean
and gravity.
There's only one problem:
with no reason to struggle
the human race would deteriorate.
So Dwayne has vowed never to reveal
the details of his creation.
It will die with him, unspoken.
He has saved mankind.

IMBECILES IN THE TORRENT

The elderly Chinese woman waits at her window
watching the rain.
She wants it to stop
so she can water her flowers.
You should hear the way
she talks to her dog, his ears
flatten and his tail
goes between his legs.
She lives alone, she drove
all her relatives away
and killed the
cat.
It's only her
and the dog now, and
the flowers.
It doesn't rain
in the desert much
and so for most of the year the flowers
need the woman to
survive.
Maybe it's the price
of independence:
to hang their heads
like imbeciles
in the torrent,
to drink until they choke
on their own color.
The old Chinese woman watches it all through
her window glass,
musty and foul,
the blooms pink as the
tongues of seagulls
in a cold and cloudy
soup.

NAKED PREGNANT EVIL CLOWN FACE

Just a regular-looking woman with a newborn,
she rolled her stroller into our photo shop
to drop off some film.
Later, when I developed the photographs,
I found every frame on the roll was a shot of her,
the very same woman,
except she was stark naked,
eight and a half months pregnant
and her face was painted
like an evil clown:
bloodless white base,
red and black around the eyes,
big orange mouth.
She had posed in what had to be
every nook and cranny
of her big Victorian house:
there was naked pregnant evil clown face
in the recliner,
there she was at the kitchen stove,
there she was by the bookshelf
and setting the table with china;
there was naked pregnant evil clown face
watching tv,
standing by the sideboard,
in the bathtub
(clouded by an irony of bubbles),
there she was on the bed
with her eyes wide open.

I saw it all:
naked pregnant evil clown face's butt,
naked pregnant evil clown face's balloons,
naked pregnant evil clown face's ratty black pom-pom
and naked pregnant evil clown face's
humongous naked belly...

When she came back in to get her developed photographs
I hardly recognized her,
she was so thin

with that rose in her cheeks
and the pastel clothing,
and the little monster in the stroller
grinning like a star.

HOT IRON

She uses a flat hot iron
to straighten her hair.
It has a porcelain handle
and burning platypus jaws
and each morning she gets up
and plugs it in the wall.
You can smell it getting hot.
Her hair is golden-
rod laughing, but her dad
told her she was ugly
and her hair was too curly
every god damned day.
It's a delicate operation:
to change who you are
without burning your scalp.
It's been eleven years
since she's seen him, calls
another country home now
but she still gets up
and plugs in her hot iron
every morning. It's ready
when your spit sizzles.

SHARON

is an old hooker, a bit heavy
and she talks too much, it's hard
to get a word in edgewise. She's pissed
because she thinks she's going to have
to go legit. She's forty-three years old,
raucous, whiskey voiced, tall and big boned,
almost sexy, always bra-less.
She's got a line and a story for everything. Funny
if you're in the mood. Anyway today she's
bitching because someone left a letter
on her doorstep which said she was
being watched. Now she's seeing
cops everywhere and she's lost her
regulars and is all in an uproar.
She admits she's getting older and fatter anyway
so maybe it's about time she turned
her life around. She's getting drunk
before she goes in to her first night
at her first real job in her entire life:
posing nude for the figure drawing class
at the college.
She's nervous about it
and I can't help it,
it touches me.

TUCSON MONSOON

The venerated rain and all of us
driving in two feet of water, children scooped

off their feet and taken laughing down the wash
which was bone dry an hour before, dogs

running around like escaped convicts, thunder like
semis crashing, the whole black lashing

mass moving toward us and over us, the rain staked
by the wind like tent ropes, enemies

smiling at each other, headlights winking in the din,
everyone helpless and giddy, where're

the wipers, where's the de-fogger, butterflies
while hydroplaning, the fever of humidity,

people yelling simply to be understood,
a billion fingers on an aluminum awning, girls pawing

their hundred dollar hair in the shrill wind,
clothes like runny paint, mother nature stripping

us raw, umbrellas like race car parachutes,
electricity, trees shaking like giant wet dogs

in slow motion, then, as suddenly as it came, the
edge of the cloud, a butt of pumpernickel,

sun rays cutting down, sovereign again, a last
grumble, the circus moving on

toward Casa Grande, toward Phoenix,
fading lightning like great pillars of neon

falling and breaking along the horizon, a rainbow,
the miracle of dragonflies...

EARLY/LATE

There's an alley
I walk through
to go to work.
This morning
I came upon
a man sleeping
there. He lay
on an old door
torn from some
abandoned house
now flat and closed
on the earth.
He had a pillow
very white in
the moonlight
of four-thirty.
His small dark
head looked
so peaceful,
I tried
to walk
without
a sound.

I STICK TO THE DAY

and the day sticks to me
like dust on sweat.
I walk the trash and tumbleweed streets
of downtown Tucson
at 3 o'clock p.m.
July 4th.
The fireworks are prepared on the
mountain
and children practice looking up
though it hurts the eyes
the sky and sun so piercing
but never perfect
always waiting and leading
into the next sky
and the next sun.
I am a different person now than I was
when I woke up this morning
alone and half buried
in the wash
and I will be another man
when I get to where I am
walking to
through this heat like the tips
of matches under my tongue
and when the night finally falls
like a false mercy
I will find a place to sit
at the foot of the mountain
and no one will
know who I am
when the darkness
explodes.

BETWEEN US AND IT

I'm a white American and she's Mexican
but we're trying to make it work.
We've moved in together.
There's a dumpster outside our bedroom window
15 feet away,
a cement block wall
between us and it.
The dumpster belongs to the other apartment building,
the last of the expensive white ones
before it turns Mexican.
At night we are startled
by people throwing things
into the dumpster.
The noises are sudden and vicious, like thunder
or war, as if they are so proud,
as if it was the surest thing in the world
to be throwing away a microwave at midnight.
Later in the night
we hear the Mexicans
taking things out of the dumpsters
to fix and resell.
The nights are hot in the desert in the summer
and in our sweaty sleep
the blanket on the bed gets pushed
and mashed together
between us.
We call it "the border".
Even on the hottest nights we can't
toss it away.

THE RUG

I bought a Persian rug
at the outdoor swap-meet.
The slick guy with the accent said
$1500 easy in a shop in L.A.
but here only $500.
I talked him down to $425.
Josie gave me her
worried flower eyes
and we hissed about it for a bit
and when she looked at the mountains
I bought it.
The guy bundled it and tied it
with a hairy twine.
In the house I cut it free
and we laid it on the floor. It didn't float
or fly, it just caught
what we tracked in, stretched out between us
and the tv.
After a few weeks we couldn't walk
on it any more
thinking of the price
so we hung it up on the wall
wrestling with the big awkward weight of it
snapping at each other until it held
and we stepped back and
stood transfixed.
Sometimes when I'm drunk or when I get up
in the middle of the night
and I see in the half-light
that rug on the wall
it is like the whole world
has tilted
fallen on its side
and I almost stagger
like a child in a fun house
only I am not
laughing,
and my bare feet are cold
on the tile.

AFTER VISITING JOSIE'S FAMILY IN MEXICO

In Hermosillo they don't have mailboxes
on the houses.
If you think something
will come in the mail
that will transform your life
like hope in a tin can
you're out of luck here.
So many Americans sit at their windows waiting
like comet freaks,
their lives dead rocks
floating around the mailbox
like a black hole on a stick.
That's why people go crazy
on Sundays.
The mailman is many people's only friend:
his predictable orbit,
his little white van like a streak in the sky.
The trick is not to worry,
that's all.
If something is meant to find you
it'll find you.
In Hermosillo,
the guy brings the electric bill
on a moped
and sticks it under your car's windshield wiper,
where your 6 year old nephew finds it
and makes a paper airplane
that sails across the bed
and pokes you in the moon.

AT THE PARK

The lady pulled her car into the parking lot
at the park, got out and opened the trunk,
took something out and walked over to the
shade under a tree, and proceeded to
put together this portable fencing which made a
kind of cage without a roof and it was maybe
eight feet by five feet and hardly big enough,
I thought, for a dog, which I assumed she was
going to put in there, and I assumed
right, only it wasn't a dog, it was *five* dogs
and not small dogs either, I don't know what
kind of dogs but medium sized dogs, I mean they
barely had room to turn around, and here
they were in this five acre park, trees to
piss on and things to sniff everywhere,
trapped in this stupid little child's playpen, and
maybe the lady had her good reasons, I'm sure
she did, and it's true the dogs didn't seem to
mind, they just plopped down and kept quiet,
apparently used to it, not thinking anything
odd about it, and in fact they could have
jumped over it if they really wanted to,
and so I really don't know why the whole
thing depressed me like it did, or why
I bother to go out into the world at all.

THE LAST WILL AND TESTICLE

I'm not gonna get that old,
the guy told me at the bar, I'm never
gonna get that way, you know,
when you can hardly walk
because you've got these hemorrhoids
hanging down like a big bunch of grapes
and when you try to talk you just
drool all over yourself
and some soft hearted social worker
has to hold a spoon of pre-masticated gruel of lima bean
out in front of yer face saying
here comes the choo-
choo train fer chrissakes.

No, not me, he said.

I was thirty years his junior
and agreed with him fully.

Then he told me about an old friend of his
who became impotent, but he was so rich
he got himself a ten thousand dollar implant
to inflate his penis into a kind of immortal
fatty. Then he drove down to Tijuana
and dallianced with a prostitute for three days straight.
He almost killed the poor girl
and he was seventy-eight years old.
He couldn't ejaculate, you see, but he didn't care.
Damn, he was a horny old bastard...

There was a place on his right hip under the skin
that he could pump with his hand
to fill the tool with some kind of artificial fluid
like those pump up basketball shoes.

When the old son of a bitch died
he expressed clearly in his will
that they were to remove the apparatus
and hand it down as an heirloom.

We sipped our beers, and then I said, I take it
you were the lucky recipient?

He smiled in the bar mirror.
Not that I'm ever gonna use it, he said,
but it did cost a lot of money, and it just doesn't seem right
to throw some things away.

THREE WEEKS I'LL NEVER GET BACK

I worked at a telephone collection agency
for three weeks.
On breaks the long term employees stood
outside and smoked
and talked about their rude behavior
and someone would always say,
"Hey, we're *collectors*,
what do you expect
from a *collector*?"
And everyone always laughed and nodded
as if it was some elite tribe of
underground geniuses
some talented mysterious substrata
tough and gritty and kind of
cool-Hollywood-hip
as if being a pasty-faced computer blob
who sat in a cubicle judging and
insulting people all
day everyday was something to be
proud of.
In much the same way every person who owed
anybody a red cent
was referred to as a *debtor*
with a disdainful tone and a bit
of saliva.
The manager was instructed to hire
"anybody who walks in the door"
but most people who answered the constant
HELP WANTED ads
ran within a few days,
some within a few hours or
minutes.
Only the real masochists stuck
around long enough
to stand outside on
smoke breaks
and brag
behind the bullet proof building.

BILL COLLECTOR

He's a real pro.
When old ladies call
to say they are dying
and have no money
he dangles the phone
over the garbage can.
One day an envelope comes
like a birthday card
with a hundred dollar bill
smeared with feces.
He's like a man leaning
too far over his cake
when the smell hits him.
It could be human
or some other animal,
you can't really tell.
But, he doesn't cry.
He goes to the bathroom
and washes it off
like chocolate from his tie.

THE BELL

There was a little bell on the boss's desk
at the collection agency
where we were paid
to telephone people
and make them feel like dog crap.
It was a bell like on a hotel counter
when the clerk's gone.
When a collector received a credit card payment
it was procedure to stand up from the little desk
and walk across the room
past all the others sitting
at their own little desks
and to place the payment slip
in the box on the boss's desk
and to tap the top
of the little bell.
The bell was intended to make us jealous
and mindlessly competitive
like posting everyone's totals
on the wall in big red numbers:
it dug into our hamster brains
and we worked harder and harder
to make the world miserable,
to make ourselves miserable.
We told mothers their sons
were losers
and we told grandmothers if they didn't
pay their bills before they died
they'd go to hell
and their families would never forgive them.
And that little bell
kept dinging
and our mouths watered
for affection.

THE JAGS

They had "his & her" Jaguars.
Hers was purple, his was yellow.
They used to come into the cheap family restaurant
where I was a waiter.
They came in every Sunday
just when it was getting weedy
and requested me.
I hated them.
I fantasized about murdering them
in those jags.
They were in their fifties.
She was of Mexican heritage,
short hair, like her head was dipped in ink.
He was white and bald as a boiled egg.
Sometimes they arrived in the yellow Jag,
sometimes the purple,
but they always parked
in the handicapped parking place right up front,
even though they both walked
like bouncing colts.
Every smile I gave them was a fake,
disgusted solicitude, an ugly matter
of survival
that I am now ashamed of.
I hated myself in those days,
and they fed on that.
I rode my bicycle to work each night
all the way from Craycroft and Twenty-Second Street
and locked it to a pipe out back.
It had one speed
and was puppy shit
green.

ON THE OTHER SIDE OF THE MOUNTAIN

His name's Banks,
65 years old, 6' 2", 190 pounds
with 648 days in Vietnam
and 50 Arizona summers
on the permanent file of his face.
He stares at two young women
who've taken the bar hostage
with their cleavage and nonstop chirping.
The other regulars attend to them
like overacting locals
in a summer stock embarrassment.
When the girls finally leave
everyone is disappointed
except Banks
who sits up a little straighter
and mutters,
"Thank god."
They say he lives
out in the county
with a small arsenal
and a gentle old dog.

WE'VE ALWAYS BEEN A FAMILY DOLLAR FAMILY

Yes, I know there are people who swear
by The Dollar Store, which is
ok I guess, you can get
some good deals sometimes, but you
see, at The Dollar Store everything really isn't a dollar.
At Family Dollar
everything's a dollar.
I think a name should reflect the
spirit of the store.
I went to Canton to visit my sister last year
and they had something called
The Dollar Tree,
but that makes you think you can just walk in
and pick money off the branches.
I remember we had a Dollar General and a Dollar Daze
once upon a time,
but they went out of business
when The 99 Cent Store
backed in.
I admit I spent a buck
or two in there, but that
was years ago, before Family Dollar came to town.
I remember the first time I walked in it
was like coming home.
I knew where everything was as if by instinct.
Everything I wanted
they had.
And yes, everything was a dollar.
And the quality of the product was astounding.
Take the Christmas tree tinsel for instance.
The quality of the Christmas tree tinsel was much better
than the tinsel you'll find at the others.
Go and find out for yourself.
Unless you're unfortunate enough not to have a Family
Dollar in your town, in which case
you're just gonna have to settle
for whatever Christmas tinsel is available.

SAM

I spent two years in Vietnam
Sam says to me at the bar.

My dad's your age, I say, but his
number never came up. He was
worried but it never came up.

I enlisted, Sam says. My brother
enlisted before me and he was only there
a month, just long enough to get
his leg blown off
and go blind.

How could you enlist after that? I say.

I don't know, he says,
I guess I wanted my revenge.

Out of the corner of my eye I look at him:
small frame, dark wrinkled face, white hair
and white beard, a few missing teeth.

Did you get it? I ask.
What? he says.

Your revenge.

I killed fifty two men, he says
with the slightest nod.

My girlfriend got a DUI the other night,
he says, it's her fifth one.
She's in jail right now.

Which one? I ask.

He looks at his beer for a minute
and says, The Indian
I think.

FRAGILE

The woman takes down the pictures of her family
and tucks them in a box.
They all look shocked
staring through their little windows
stiff as the sweater people
in the Sears newspaper insert
lining the bottom.

She crumples up
the headlines, stuffs them between
their sharp-elbowed frames
and wraps the whole thing
thoroughly as a headwound.

She tries to protect them
with the magic wand
of her black marker
but she knows too well the way

things shift, and crack;
and the way water always seeps in
like amnesia.

THE BUFFET TAVERN, TUCSON, ARIZONA

Don't go spouting transcendentalism.
Don't go spouting anything.
Just go and listen:
listen to Viking Mike talk
about sleeping in the bush,
listen to diesel-mouth Bill talk about his rig,
listen to Dirk
(who looks like Rasputin)
talk about his ex-wife's suicide,
listen to Jimmy Reed slop
his heart out,
listen to Daddy Treetops with his tennis elbow
and to Dan the cab driver
with his gravedigger's fingernails
and to old Tom in his wheelchair
with a napkin for his drool,
listen to the Dragon Lady
with her wine and
shedding forearms...
The tavern opens at six a.m.
just like a bakery,
and there's always a line at the door in the dark
waiting for their jolly loaves.
Go,
but be careful:
that place eats people
like you and me.

TRASH

I used to burn the trash after dinner.
We lived in the country.
In the twilight
I would walk out to the back yard
toss the paper sack
into the rusted-out blackened barrel
seeing a few things
against my will:
chicken bones,
sister's tampon,
envelopes bills came in
and I would take a match
to something thin
watch it blaze up
throwing warmth.
I had to step away a couple of feet
when it got too hot.
I would stay until the flames
died down
and I shivered
then I'd walk back
to the house
to the blue light
of the television
and the cold white
faces.

THE COPPERHEAD AND THE BLUE FLOWER

I'm six years old
and I want that blue flower
hanging there.
I step off the gravel road
into the weeds, reach up the vine
and bring it in,
warping the sky.
When I have it I am satisfied
but then I look down:
a copperhead snake
is zeroed in on my bare foot,
flicking its tongue
red as my heart,
red as a minnow
with its face cut open.
I wait a few seconds,
growing all the time,
expecting to die...
But, somehow,
it does not strike,
and because of this I understand
I am free.
I slowly back away
with my blue flower
coiled in my hand,
balancing on one foot,
then the other.

BAD SUMMER

We killed fourteen copperhead snakes
one summer.

My dad helped me skin one
and make a hat band
for my black cowboy hat.

I remember a fat one
I slit at the belly
(as my mother looked on)
and out squirmed a spaghetti mess
of baby snakes
slimy and bloody
but alive.

We didn't know what else to do
but feed them
to the fire.

HALF DRUNK IN THE AFTERNOON

I'm sitting on the patio
of a neighborhood bar

when a paramedic truck roars up.
The story rushes by on the breeze:

the heat has caused a woman to collapse
somewhere down the trail

that runs along the dry river bed.
People have stopped

and are pointing from the bridge
into the glare.

I WISH I HAD SOME ROPE

The first time Kim cheated on me
she had to offer all the sordid details:
he whispered in her ear while he mounted how he wished
he had some rope to bind her arms
(it didn't matter that he didn't have any
like it didn't matter that she didn't
want to like it but did).

They were in a college play together.
I went to rehearsal that night
and sat way up in the bleachers
where they could see me from the stage.
He was a real pro
and I kept thinking
"I wish I had some rope for you."

He came up to me when it was over.
He knew who I was.
We went outside and stood under a tree
big enough to block the moon.
I told him to stay away from her
and very quietly he promised he would
and for some reason I believed him.
I don't know if it was true.

He walked away
and I went to Kim at her apartment
where we screamed until we cried.

That was 25 years ago
and to be fair I should say I did
my share of sleeping around on her too
and I gave her plenty of gory details
and I created my share of dramatics.

We dated for 3 years after that night
before breaking up for good one winter day
outside an abortion clinic in St. Louis
for an angry audience
of picketers.

COUNTY

I was in jail for a month.
I was amazed at how much fun
my fellow inmates could have.
Once a week we were marched down to a room
the size of half a basketball court
and ordered to exercise.
There was a basketball backboard
painted on the wall, but no hoop
and no ball. One time
the inmates started playing football
with twenty socks rolled up together
and soon they were having such a good time
that the guards ordered everyone
to surrender their socks.

I remember the stupid, pulpy hatred
on the faces of those guards
as if we were the worst
possible waste of human life.
I wanted to kill them, honestly,
but what bothered me most
was that no one else did.

Instead of getting angry
they just started
playing soccer
with their rubber slippers.

BOO

I remember when you put in that cat door
for Boo.
It was funny to watch him sniff it
and jump when we messed
with the rubber flap.
Finally he just nosed out
and you praised him in that baby voice
until I wanted to slap you.

We never thought it could work both ways
but a stray cat came in one day
while we were at work
and had kittens in the closet.
We let her stay
and when the kittens were old enough to give away
I had to corner her
with a blanket
and I can say with honesty
I've seen a cat climb plaster walls.
We took them all out to a farm you knew of.

And then after we broke up
Boo disappeared
from the sidewalk right outside your window
and you finally just
moved away.

Everybody blamed it on a coyote or an owl
but people are stupid when it comes to blame.

NEW YEAR'S EVE

Jim and Sue have a fight
and Jim walks out the back door
and sets off the alarm.
After Sue turns the alarm off

she walks back to the helium tank
and rips an empty balloon out.
The tank whines and the balloon swells
and when you think it'll explode

she takes it off and ties it
at the throat with deaf fingers.
She gives the balloon to George
who walks it to the dance floor

and lets it go against the ceiling
with the others bumping each other
like dumb ghosts, cartoon sperm
dangling tails without faces.

Jim never comes back
and the crowd never forms
and later when some asshole pops
a balloon with a clove cigarette

Sue jumps three feet in the air
and starts crying silently.
It's another perfect holiday
for all of us down here in Dirt City.

THINGS CAN BE BEAUTIFUL
EVEN WHEN THEY'RE NOT

After dreaming a homeless dream
of good men going bad with the
frequency of leaves falling, I wake
to find dreams funny
only because I don't understand them,

and I sit by the window in all this unknowing
and I see
the lore of degenerate tulips,
the magnificent overcrowding of space
and mystery,
and some gothic Stonehenge figure is mowing the lawn
and my landlady wanders the halls in
Palestine robes
and Martians skittle over the sidewalks wearing headphones
and morning pulls on the cape of night.

I faint from the boredom and fatigue
and disbelief
and I march my dummies one by one
over the cliff of my refusal.
What, really, is there to know or
to say?

The church on the corner is a big dumb paperweight
resting on an old fool's map
and when god breathes
deep,
the candles barely flicker,

and the doctors are telling us what to read before bed
and the fishermen smell their fingers
and sigh
and the busses are full of sullen youths
staring at their one hundred dollar shoes.

In the dream I move from place to place
with too many belongings

and nowhere to rest
except the flower bed
(things can be beautiful even when they're not real)

and I am being stepped on by Terror's foot
and falling I kiss the earth
and I lay on the ground sinking
and the small animals see me
and run away.

WE HAVE SEEN IT FOR SO LONG

As the day is imperfect
I am imperfect
as all opposites
bellow for freedom
and then holler loneliness
or boredom
the moon means so much to us
because we have seen it for so long
as the world bucks and postures
and wriggles for air I grab at
things like a child
running after lightning bugs
with a whisky bottle
while toads hop at my feet
and men and women scream through
splintered doorways
and the night smashes like shame
against the earth and stars
war in a small boy's heart
and the creek and the cool air murmur
of the tadpole with two heads
the crawdad with one claw
the lizard missing a tail
all precaution and chance thrown
like a can of beer by
every father filled
with hatred and frustration
because of mistakes
that will not matter
in the end.

GERTRUDE THE GOOD

Gertrude lives with us here
at Park Vista Apartments.
She's eighty-six years old with one eye
black and drooping,
a nose like an old man's penis
and a mouth that will not close
nor a tongue that will stay in her mouth
as she moves slowly around the parking lot
leaking her opinions from a beat-
up old aluminum walker.

Today we are all waiting for the mail
and when it finally comes
the only thing each one of us gets
(despite friendly banter with the mailman)
is a measly catalogue for
garden supplies.
None of us has a yard, not even a solitary
aspidistra flying,
just cinder block and iron bars and bad dreams.
We all just toss the catalogues
into the garbage bin
muttering disappointment.

All except Gertrude.
Gertrude holds her catalogue
and exclaims in glee.
She scoots her walker back
through the gravel to her stinky hot
single-room apartment where she drags
a chair outside and
reads that catalogue cover
to cover
all afternoon
smiling the whole time
with her tongue
falling out
like a cocker spaniel.

LA DUEÑA

One day someone delivered a decorative plant
to my boss, the owner of Casa Molina
and it was left on the bar.
It had big pink and blue flowers
and all the waitresses and waiters
thought it was beautiful.
We watered it and picked off the dead leaves
and it made it slightly more tolerable
slopping enchiladas and
margaritas to the college alumni.
My boss never puts a dime
into that place
and she thinks the proper way to run things
is to come in twice a day
and rip the staff new assholes.
The restaurant stays afloat
because of the reputation of her dead husband
and the hard work of Mexican immigrants
who she treats like farm animals.
She was a Mexican immigrant herself
but that's different.
One day she noticed we were
enjoying that plant she left on the bar.
She suddenly remembered it was hers
and took it and left it by the
back loading door
in order to take it home later that night.
That was a month ago.
I noticed it today
sitting in the place
where she left it
brown and crisp and dead, an example
for us all.

4 AMERICAN MEN SIT AT THE CAMPGROUND PICNIC TABLE DRINKING BEER

A young slim girl
in tight denim shorts
walks past them and enters
the midwest summer campground bathroom
where she arranges
a perfect face
in the smudged metal mirror
and dreams of some far away city
that will love her.
She hates her parents and walks back out
past the men again
who are all married
to old wives as easy
and plain as local
anesthetics.
As the vixen smiles
they barely hold their jaws up
above the piss colored seltzer
of their domestic beers.
She walks away and they have to wrench
themselves to keep from staring,
sit riveted like wing nuts to their seats.
When she is gone the men convulse
like fat genies
have given them a gift
rubbing beer bottles and shaking bellies
swollen from
what has already come true,
what can only come true once.

BULIMIA

Her arms are origami,
her head totters on a toy neck
and her back is bowed
like a bone violin.
She wants to be loved
for who she is,
for what she is inside:
she wants to be pure soul
but it's all inseparable
and her soul is fading away
like her flesh,
like her gums and hair and teeth,
her ribs poking out
like an animal that's traveled too far,
like some child or saint or martyr
who would crumble
if I tickled her.
When we hug goodbye
she's so tiny
it's like she's a part of me:
my hands reach all the way around her
and touch the soft
tender places
under my arms.

THIS GIRL

was in the bookstore today
where I went to escape
the heat.

She was holding her cell phone
not talking into it
just taking the antenna
in and out
with her teeth.

Every once in a while
there was a flash
of tongue.

She was just absently
doing this
while looking at
a row of books
and leaning on
one
hip.

It was damn
sexy.

She didn't
even know what
she was doing

or maybe she
did.

She couldn't
have
been older than fourteen.

It's a crazy
stupid
world.

HOT AIR BALLOON RIDE

In that five-foot-wide four-foot-deep basket
the pilot and his wife argued
for the whole forty-five minutes.
It was just the four of us:
Josie and I pressed against
the thin wall of the basket
roped our fingers together and looked
as far away as we could.
The farms were laid out all around
like a sheet of stamps.
The pilot made the fire roar
to drown out the sound of their angry voices
and in this way the fuel
was spent early.
We were all sweating.
This is what they do:
travel from town to town
hauling that huge balloon
unrolling it and rolling it back up
for twenty years.
On the way back to earth
we barely missed some power lines
and descended into a herd
of scattering cows.
The woman walked across the pasture crying.
The man drew out
a lukewarm bottle of champagne
popped it
and filled our plastic glasses.
He made an apology for a toast
and then asked if we wanted a photo taken
for five bucks.

BATH DAY

After we got electricity
once a week we heated water
in big pots on the stove
and poured it
into the old bathtub my dad found
at the dump.

It took 3 pots
for 6 inches of water
which was all we got
and the water was never very hot
by that time.

Me and my sister shared the same water.
We took turns going first.

Then my mom got her own water
which took another hour to fill.

My dad didn't have the patience.
He bathed in the creek
all winter long
where the water ran fast enough
to prevent freezing.

You could hear him hollering down there
like a sick bear.

We laughed so hard
it almost
kept us warm.

SPRING IS IN THE AIR

Dad de-balls the Billy goat
this bullfrog morning.
His horns are coming in—
bleeding something awful.
Dad ties him up upside down
braying and bucking
like the dark-haired girl
from The Rusty Nail,
while mom wrings her
apron in the doorway.
Blood drips as the kid screams
like a child who'd fuck
his own mother. Goat milk
is sour, and the meat
will stick to your bones.

THE STRAYS

The dying white kitten
trembles in the shade of the lime tree
with a mosquito sucking its nose.
I set a bowl of milk down
but he just moves painfully away
yellow shit matted up and down his tail.
His mother has two others she attends to
leaving the white one
to die alone.
There was a fourth kitten
a black one
but one day I got in my car and
a block later looked back in my
mirror and there it was
twitching and stumbling on the road.
He had been hiding underneath my car
and when I turned a corner he was thrown out
and mutilated.
His eye was out of its socket
as he tried to stand up
and fell
and tried again and
fell again.
I watched him die
so quiet and brave
and I put him on the side of the road
ashamed.
Now the white one is dying
from what I don't know
and there's a mosquito on its nose
and those yellow eyes look at me
so sadly
and the two
that are still healthy
seem so stupid and
lucky
and I do not
like them.

DEEDER OF THE DAMNED

Deeder was a six-foot-four fire hydrant
with ice water blood.
He was kicked off the high school football team
for being too rough,
then expelled from school for ripping out a urinal
and threatening to shit
down the principal's neck.
But he stuck around town.
He lived on the street or in the slammer.
Once he killed a police dog
by shoving his fist down its throat.
Deeder never carried a weapon
or raised his voice
but if you dialed 9-1-1 and whispered his name
the cops showed up in minutes.
For what seemed like forever
Deeder haunted the streets,
taverns and nightclubs
with his black eyes and cold brow.
The other day he was found dead:
shot in a hotel room.
Maybe the cops did it,
maybe a drug deal went sour,
who knows.
The truth is as slippery
as an ice cube on a bar top. All I know is
that night we all drank
to a good long life
and then walked home in the dark
feeling strangely empty.

IT SEEMS IMPOSSIBLE

Harold is the head librarian at the Wilmot prison
and over beers at El Corral he tells me
a female co-worker fucked
an inmate in the library,
a guy doing time for rape.
The woman was fired but she waited for
the inmate's release
and then she married him.
They live in Colorado now
and have to tell the cops every
time they move.
It seems impossible but people who know them
say they're happy.
Harold gets loud and
angry as he tells me about it
and I wonder why it bothers him so much,
and I wonder why it bothers me.
"Fuckin bitch," he mutters.
He shakes his head and
turns to his wife
as if there is plexiglass
between them.

ON THE CORNER OF MAPLE AND EUCLID

It's a bright day in May
and a cop car screams past
the run-down little house.
In the yard a girl and boy
throw their hands to their ears
and stand and stare at each other
with their mouths open,
like little red suns.
Their mother comes to the door
in wet yellow gloves
thinks of her husband,
and how twenty years really is
the same as life.
The old man on the porch
opens frightened eyes
from a rocking chair dream.
The dog runs to the end of the chain
                        and howls.

ONCE YOU'VE PAID

for the same call-girl
four or five times
you throw the rules out.
After a grand or more you're going
to kiss her on the
mouth if you feel like it
(trying not to think
about all those other cocks)
and you're going to take her
twice maybe
and you're going to explore
her ass
and you're going to stretch it out
longer than an hour sometimes.
Once you've seen her a few times
you get to know things
like how many kids she has
what she did before this
how she keeps it
from her family. You learn her
real name and the nature
of her soft spots, her hair roots,
her failed plans and her new ones.
Of course by this time you get
tired of her
or you feel she's taking advantage of you
or your money peters out
and one day you just stop calling her.
Because she is a prostitute
there is no break up,
which is a ritual governed
by another set of rules
and another set of women,
rules which can be thrown out only at the price
of respectable life
in respectable society,
which is getting off
cheap
if
you ask me.

JAMIE

I remember the summery
small of a back
a long Mongolian
stare
buttermilk arms.

I remember breasts
high as snowtop
lips that kissed
and ate the air
cheekbones
that rose like sharks.

And especially I remember
two eyes
like trapped butterflies
shoulders like
the softest crystal balls

and the tiniest feet
like exotic birds
that would never quite eat
from my hands.

OUTHOUSE

Grasshoppers leap against the wooden walls
like locusts
some getting through the cracks
spitting
their green blood.

She can't breathe.
She kicks the door open, legs shackled
by blue jeans and belt.

Beads of sweat cling to her
like transparent eggs.

On invisible rising currents
vultures circle above,
bloody tampons dangling from their beaks.

THE MINUTES TIGHT WITH REPENTANCE

Shamed
into peace
I hear footsteps

then a strange key
in my lock
my deep cold copper heart

we both wait
not breathing
six inches from each other

finally
the fading
of footsteps

something is locked in
each minute
that ticks by

each breath like a stroke
toward the middle
of the ocean

TONYA WEISS

She's seventeen years old
and at midnight
she falls through the high school gym skylight
into the dark
like a hard swallow.

The next morning
she is found
on the parquet floor—

the same floor
where the cheerleaders dance
at home games

where we play dodge ball
like killers

where we do wind sprints
until our guts heave.

MY LAST LUCKY PENNIES

I hurt myself planting yellow squash.
It's too late into the season
and I've never done it before
but my girlfriend encouraged me
and I do think buttery squash is like
licking your love's fingers.
I had to dig through the desert soil
in back of our apartment
which is nothing but clay and gravel
and construction backfill.
I struck into it with my spade
and churned it up
chinking like a man slowly working away
at a pair of iron ankle-cuffs.
Finally I had a little plot
big as a dog's grave
and I added manure and fertilizer
and I dropped those squash seeds there
like my last lucky pennies.
Now I'm in bed with
a hurt neck.
Every time I move my head to the side
I have shooting sparks
like that spade hitting flint.
Those little fucking squash
better come up,
I swear to God,
and they better look like roses.

SHOOTING THE CHICKENS

My dad can't answer their eyes
when he axes their heads off

so he stands at the thin edge
of the yard where they run free,

one eye closed, left shoulder
hefting the rifle, forefinger

beckoning till it's blue. No
clouds, but the thunder and lightning

drop the birds like civilians,
faces pressed into the mirrors

of their own pooling blood,
quiet among the poor clucks

of the still living. We say fuck
plucking them, instead hang

them by their feet and pull
their skin down whole to find

out who they really are,
before devouring them.

DRIVING HOME FROM MY MOM'S FUNERAL

A black cable lays across the street
to record how many pass.

It reminds me of that black snake that stretched
all the way across our gravel road

when I was a kid in Arkansas.
Even though we were leaving

the farm and dad and everything,
mom stopped the truck in tears

and we sat and waited
for it to cross. Thirty years later

I drive over it. There is no choice,
only two hard heartbeats

and a still line
in the rearview mirror.

AN ANGEL IN AN ANKLE BRACELET

I have bars on my window.
It's that kind of neighborhood.
The woman who lives across the alley
is under house arrest.
Having few outward liberties
she has turned her back yard
into a paradise.
It's a pure botanical event
riotous as a prison break
with flowers and grasses
and vines and all kinds
of green magic straining
to be free of the earth.
She is unable to go anywhere
but is still very much alive,
so she hoes and weeds and waters
and weeds and waters and hoes
day in, day out, week after week,
regular as the sun.
Through the window bars
I watch the white birds crisscross
like spotlights over her head,
an angel in an ankle bracelet
making rainbows with a garden hose.

GONE

In my apartment building
there is a tendency for people
to suddenly move out
in the middle of the night
usually leaving a bunch of crap behind
but no explanation or
goodbye.

This morning there's a big pile
on the sidewalk:
clothes, pots, pans,
collapsed boxes, cans of food,
bug infested rugs, a broken chair,
magazines, shoes.

I don't know if it
was Crutch Boy
or the lady who smells like cat urine
or the lumberjack guy
who whispers to himself

or maybe it was the little
white Buddhist kid
who sits cross-legged on his floor all day
and then limps to the mailbox

or maybe it was that hot
girl with the baby
or the cranky drunk in the corner unit
or the old woman who stands
naked at her window

or maybe it was Equity
or Sally or John Harvey
or Ernesto
or maybe it was the couple who fights
or maybe it was
poor dumb Longstreet.

I really don't
know who it was
but somebody's
gone.

THANKSGIVING 2002

I forgive the operator
and wait for the ring.
I ignore my genetic invoices,
the school of piranhas in the sink
and the bottom feeders
circling the toilet bowl.
I ignore St. Nick's holding pattern
over the chicken coop,
the desires caught
in grandfather clauses,
all these miles
of narcissism.
I ignore the old potter
burping at the wheel,
the long sleep of the turkey,
the turnkey flattened on the railroad track
and the great riverbank
of never.
Finally, his voice...
I talk to my father
for the first time
in fourteen years,
and he asks me when I'm coming home.

THAT SWEET PLACE

Señorita,
the way you looked at me
told me it would be
a long,
tongue-dry journey
to meet you half way,
and I wanted to be with you
right there, right then
forever.
As if it could ever
be so easy,
as if we could suddenly
arrive
at that sweet
place
where language is
unnecessary.
As if there was another
way to get there
besides riding
for years
on the backs
of words.

FAMILY TREE

Me and Josie go to Agua Caliente park
and look at a giant mesquite tree
bigger than I've ever seen
sprawling with great old growth grotesquely gothic arms
spidering out like a nightmare.
It's so big it would have died long ago
fallen from its own weight
and rotted into the ground
if people hadn't built a support system
of ropes and chains and rubber hoses and hammocks
and crutches to hold up the biggest
most cumbersome branches.
There's something obscene about it,
like a man grown so fat
he can't get out of bed.
Josie tries to imagine something like this happening
in Mexico where she was born.
The American fondness for animals and trees
is a strange sentimental concept to her.
And I think, Why this tree
when so many thousands of other old growth mesquites
were slaughtered seventy five years ago
so people could move in and eventually
yearn for the past?
Me and Josie both wonder if it wouldn't be better
to let it die
but we are not sure,
and so we just stand there looking at it
eating bananas.

SCUBA DIVING
IN LA PAZ

We had never done it before
and after a 15 min. lesson in broken English
we fell backwards into the water
and immediately began looking for each other.

Your shell pink bikini flashed at me,
your dark hair rose,
and the pirate's coins of your eyes
winked green from behind your mask.
Our bodies were both weightless
and heavy,
skin pale and pruny in the bath-rippled light,
hearts racing with our lungs' need,
deliberate breath, clenched jaws,
claustrophobia,
quiet as a cough syrup dream.

Great molars of rock sleeping on the bottom.

At one point something went wrong with my suit
and I lifted
helpless as a bubble
and when you couldn't find me
you came up screaming my name.

You refused to dive any more after that,
and it made me uneasy
the way the captain used his hands
when he helped you onto the deck,
the way your hair
stuck to your face like seaweed.

I am so sorry,
I realize now I shouldn't have left you
to go down again
just to see an old rusty boat
fake-sunk for the tourists

and a tiny blowfish
that appeared to be terrified,
not of me,
but of something
behind me,
coming for the both of us.

THE YEAR OF THE MOREL

Every spring we'd go mushrooming for morels,
big wrinkly things
like cone-head brains on stems.
Usually they were about 4 or 5 inches tall
and a couple inches wide,
but one time my dad came home
from a solitary expedition
and he had a morel mushroom
over a foot tall.
We took a picture of it next
to his drafting ruler.
That was 35 years ago.
I asked him about it on the phone
yesterday.
"Where's that picture gone to?"
"Lost," he said.
"I've never seen anything like it," I said.
"Me neither," he said.
He still lives in Illinois and still goes
mushrooming every spring,
but says each year
they get smaller and smaller.
I wonder if anyone
will believe me: that mushroom
was over a foot tall,
and at least 6 inches wide.
It was a monster.
This was the last year
we were all still together.
My mom cut it up and rolled it in crumbs
and fried it,
and we ate it, like that,
as a family.

TEN YEARS AWAY

I come home to find my cousin Todd
won't take his Lithium,
my mother has a tissue box
in every corner of her house
and nothing but a police scanner for company,
my niece Kim has taken too many vacations
with the Rainbow People
and is now able to communicate with cats and marigolds,
my old girlfriend Shell Macintire is now a mad
drunken nurse who hates people and breaks
dinnerware at parties,
our old house is all grown up
with vines and mean-looking grasses
and there are cages of angry dogs behind the shed
where I opened my first nudie mag,
most of the good looking girls from high school
are a mess
and a couple of the homely ones
have found their own
and most of them have been divorced at least once,
the bridge is out down
by Johnson's Hollow
and the lake where I used to skinny dip
with Theresa Ozuna
has been drained,
there's a new road to my grandpa's old house
out in the woods,
but it still looks rough,
it still looks plenty rough back there.

Mather Schneider was born in 1970 in Peoria, Illinois. His previous works include *Poormouth* (Interior Noise Press; 2003) and *Hell Traits: Poems from the Old Pueblo* (Temporary Vandalism; 2008). He currently resides in Tucson, Arizona.

The author gratefully acknowledges the following publications in which many of these poems first appeared:

Abbey
Atlanta Review
Black Book Press
Bolts of Silk
Breadcrumb Scabs
Buzzard Picnic
Calliope Nerve
Chiron Review
Fight These Bastards
Gutter Eloquence
Hanging Loose
Ink, Sweat & Tears
Left Behind
Lit Up Magazine
Maelstrom
My Favorite Bullet
Nerve Cowboy
Nimrod
Poetry Warrior
Poor Mojo's Almanac
PS Highway
Rattle
RHINO
River Styx
Rumble
Ship of Fools
Shoots and Vines
Silt Reader
Sow's Ear
Staple Gun
The Laughing Dog
The Ledge
Thorny Locust
Underground Voices
Veil Magazine
Why Vandalism?
ZZZ Zyne

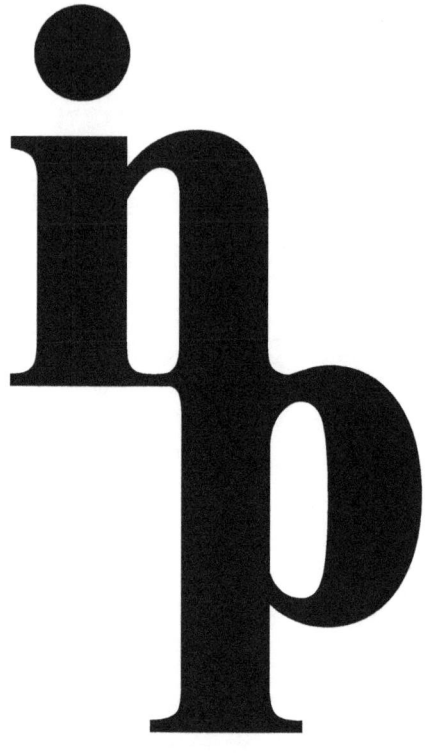

www.interiornoisepress.com

www.ingramcontent.com/pod-product-compliance
Lightning Source LLC
Chambersburg PA
CBHW020941090426
42736CB00010B/1215